TAKE ACTION SAVE LIFE ON EARTH

SAVE NATIVE PLANTS

Stephanie Feldstein

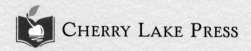

CHERRY LAKE PRESS

Published in the United States of America by Cherry Lake Publishing Group
Ann Arbor, Michigan
www.cherrylakepublishing.com

Reading Adviser: Beth Walker Gambro, MS, Ed., Reading Consultant, Yorkville, IL
Book Designer: Felicia Macheske

Photo Credits: TK © mark wilson 9119/Shutterstock, cover; © Eduardo Ramirez Sanchez/Shutterstock, 5; © Mark Baldwin/Shutterstock, 9; © Paul Reeves Photography/Shutterstock, 11; © Erik Agar/Shutterstock, 13; © My Good Images/Shutterstock, 14; © Danita Delimont/Shutterstock, 17; © Ammit Jack/Shutterstock, 18; © Claremont Graduate University, 21; © Pressmaster/Shutterstock, 23; © 1000 Words/Shutterstock, 24; © Beekeepx/Shutterstock, 27; © Asaylee/Shutterstock, 31; © Teerachai_P/Shutterstock, back cover; © Flower Studio, / Shutterstock, back cover

Graphics Credits: © raisin_ka/Shutterstock; © Pavel K/Shutterstock; © Panimoni/Shutterstock; © Hulinska Yevheniia Shutterstock; (All) © Vector Place/Shutterstock; | © Happy Art/Shutterstock; © Robert Adrian Hillman/Shutterstock; © DStarky/Shutterstock

Cherry Lake Press is an imprint of Cherry Lake Publishing Group.

Library of Congress Cataloging-in-Publication Data has been filed and is available at catalog.loc.gov.

Cherry Lake Publishing Group would like to acknowledge the work of the Partnership for 21st Century Learning, a Network of Battelle for Kids. Please visit *http://www.battelleforkids.org/networks/p21* for more information.

Printed in the United States of America
Corporate Graphics

Note from publisher: Websites change regularly, and their future contents are outside of our control. Supervise children when conducting any recommended online searches for extended learning opportunities.

Table of Contents

INTRODUCTION

Plants and the Extinction Crisis

High in the mountains, the soil is thin and rocky. Winter brings harsh storms. There isn't much rain in the summer. Few plants and animals can survive here. This is where whitebark pine trees grow. They can be found in many places. One of these places is the Rocky Mountains. They're also in the Cascade Mountains. Lastly, they're found in the Sierra Nevada Mountains. Whitebark pines are tough. But they're threatened with **extinction**.

Extinction is when all of one kind of plant or animal dies. It affects wild plants and animals. An extinct plant or animal is gone forever. Scientists say we're in an extinction **crisis**. When wildlife goes extinct, it weakens **ecosystems**. Healthy ecosystems provide food, shelter, water, and clean air. Life on Earth needs all kinds of plants and animals.

Native plants are a natural part of an ecosystem. Plants and animals in an ecosystem have a special relationship. At least 13 species of birds eat whitebark pine seeds. The seeds help fatten

up grizzly bears for the long winter. The trees provide shelter for animals. The seeds help other trees grow in the mountains. We need to save native plants to save ecosystems.

Two out every five wild plants are in danger. Wild plants are uprooted when wilderness is turned into farms. They're paved over for roads and buildings. They're destroyed by mining and logging. They're poisoned to make room for crops. They're harmed by **climate change**. They're exposed to diseases introduced by people.

We can stop the extinction crisis. People like us need to take action. Governments and communities need to act, too. By working together, we can save native plants.

Why We Need NATIVE PLANTS

Plants have been on Earth for millions of years. All life on Earth needs plants. Native plants support **biodiversity**. They make it possible for lots of different plants and animals to live.

Native plants create **habitat**. Habitat is the place where wild animals live. Animals use branches, leaves, and moss for nests. Roots prevent **erosion**. Erosion is when the land gets worn away. Erosion makes life harder for plants and animals. Plants provide food from their roots to leaves. **Pollinators** drink from flowers. Dead plants create healthy soil. Plants help clean the air. They make oxygen and fight climate change.

Humans need plants to survive. Thousands of different plants are used for medicine. People eat wild plants. Crops grown on farms came from wild plant relatives. We use wood to build our homes. People burn wood to cook and stay warm. Many fabrics are made from parts of plants.

Plants are part of cultural traditions. They add beauty and color to our world.

CHAPTER ONE

Barren Landscapes

Humans have changed more than 70 percent of Earth's land. People use land in many ways that hurt native plants. Mining and drilling tear up the land. Logging for wood destroys forests.

Agriculture is the biggest threat to forests and prairies. It's responsible for 80 percent of **deforestation**. Deforestation is when forests are cut down. More than one-third of the world's forests have been destroyed. That's an area twice as big as the United States. Prairies are plowed down when crops are planted. Tallgrass prairies have more than 300 different kinds of grasses and wildflowers. Only 4 percent of tallgrass prairies are left.

The Shoe Factory Road Prairie Nature Preserve in Illinois is a small example of tallgrass prairie that has been saved.

TURNING POINT

People have always tried to grow the biggest and tastiest plants. They chose the best seeds to grow. This type of seed breeding made agriculture possible. It gave us common foods like corn and apples. But in the 1970s, scientists went further. They didn't just choose the plants they wanted. They started to use technology to create them. This technology is called **genetic engineering**.

These scientists made crops that could survive certain **toxic pesticides**. About 40 percent of farmland in the United States is used to grow these crops. The fields are sprayed with more of these pesticides. They won't kill the engineered crops. But native plants and animals die. Toxic chemicals get in water and soil. Farmworkers are exposed to the poison.

The most widely used pesticide is sprayed on engineered corn and soybeans. It's also sprayed on engineered canola, cotton, and alfalfa. It kills milkweed. Milkweed is

Monarch butterfly caterpillars eat only milkweed. This is part of the reason monarch butterflies are endangered.

the only food monarch caterpillars eat. They can't grow into butterflies without it. The loss of milkweed puts monarch butterflies at risk of extinction. This one pesticide harms more than 1,600 plants and animals.

Four companies make most of the pesticides used in the world. They also produce 60 percent of the seeds used by farmers. It's a dangerous relationship. It harms wildlife. It puts farm workers and food at risk. But people are trying to change that. More farmers are growing food without pesticides. They're using a bigger variety of seeds. They're protecting native plants. More people are buying **organic** food. Organic crops are grown without toxic chemicals.

Pesticides are chemicals made to kill things like weeds or bugs that farmers don't want on fields. But they also kill important wildlife. Native plants are poisoned. Animals that eat those plants are exposed to the chemicals. They lose their food source when the plants die.

Crops can't replace native plants. They aren't part of an ecosystem. They're grown to feed or be used by people. Huge amounts of crops are grown to feed pigs, chickens, and cows. Habitat is turned into pasture for grazing. Much prairie land is turned into pasture for grazing cattle. Some people think cattle is an **invasive species**. Invasive species are plants or animals that don't belong in an ecosystem. They harm native wildlife.

Weeds are wild plants that grow where people don't want them. They sprout on farms and in gardens. People use pesticides to kill these plants. Some weeds are invasive species. They harm crops and ecosystems.

But many weeds are important to nature. Native weeds provide food for wildlife. They support biodiversity. Native plants are also good for farms and gardens. They attract pollinators. They help create rich soil. They prevent erosion. Weeds can be part of healthy ecosystems.

Invasive species are also spread by people bringing plants to ecosystems where they don't belong. They bring invasive plants for gardens. These plants may carry diseases. The invasive seeds and diseases can spread. They kill off native plants.

Climate change makes these problems worse. Extreme storms can harm plants. Warmer temperatures can change growing seasons. It's hard for plants to adapt. The whole ecosystem suffers when plants are in trouble.

◀ Cleaning your hiking shoes before and after you hike can help prevent spreading invasive seeds.

CHAPTER TWO

Grow Support for Local Plants

Helping native plants starts at home. Ask your parents if you can start a native plant garden. Research native plants in your area. Learn which plants are invasive species. Let your native garden grow wild. Watch to see the different kinds of plants that grow there. Look for pollinators and other wildlife enjoying your garden.

Keep your garden organic. That means you don't use any chemicals on it. Ask your neighbors to stop using pesticides, too. If they spray their yards, the chemicals can drift to your garden. They can drift to native plants.

A native wildflower garden can attract animals in search of food.

More than three million kinds of plants and animals live in the Amazon rainforest. It has more than 2,500 kinds of trees. There's no other place like it in the world. But it's being destroyed. Trees are cut down for logging. It's burned to make room for cattle and crops. It's ruined for drilling and mining.

Indigenous people live in the Amazon, too. Their home is being destroyed. Their cultures are in danger of being lost. But they protect the forest. Indigenous territories have 50 percent less deforestation than other areas. Protecting Indigenous rights helps protect the Amazon.

Protect native plants everywhere you go. Stay on trails so you don't step on sensitive plants. Notice different flowers and plants around you. You can take a photo or draw them to look them up at home. But don't pick them. It may not seem like much to pick a few flowers. But if everyone did it, there wouldn't be any left.

We need plants for healthy ecosystems. But plants don't get nearly as much attention as animals. Talk to other people about native plants. Share what you've learned. Tell them why plants are so important. Teach them how to notice the different kinds of plants that share our world.

CONSERVATION CHAMPION

Naomi Fraga is a professor of **botany**. She teaches people about plants. She also works in the field to save native plants. **Conservation** is action to protect wildlife and nature. Fraga restores habitat. She gets rid of invasive species. She helped protect a rare wildflower threatened by mining.

One of her jobs is to oversee the seed bank at the California Botanic Garden. A seed bank is a backup plan for plants. Seeds are dried and stored in freezers. They can stay alive for hundreds of years. They can be planted in the future if something happens to the plants in the wild.

Fraga works with a team to collect seeds from the wild. They take samples from lots of different plants. They clean and count the seeds. They make sure they're properly stored in foil envelopes. Then the seeds are put in the freezers. They're kept safe in case they're needed. The seeds also help Fraga and her team learn more about the plants. This helps them know how to protect them in the wild. The bank has seeds from more than 2,000 kinds of native plants. That's almost 30 percent of the known plants in California. They hope to save seeds from every known plant in the state.

Fraga loves plants. She's learned a lot from plants surviving in the wild. She works to save native plants so other people can learn from them, too.

CHAPTER THREE

Seeding the Future

The best way to save native plants is to save their habitat. That means ending deforestation. It means saving grasslands and stopping desert plants from being harmed. We can also give land back to nature. We can replant native plants.

Many people are working to rebuild habitat where it's been lost. It's not just about planting trees. Tree-planting projects often fail. Sometimes people plant the wrong kind of trees. Or they plant trees during the wrong season. Plants need the right conditions to grow. Ecosystems are sensitive. But restoring nature can be done right.

If you plant a tree, pick one that is native to where you live.

23

Grass seeds were brought to the United States from Europe. Neat lawns were a sign of wealth. But they take away from nature. The grasses planted in lawns are invasive species. They're also **monocultures**. That means only one type of crop is planted. They're usually sprayed with pesticides to kill weeds. They don't provide food or shelter for wildlife. There's no biodiversity.

People are bringing back native plants to where they used to grow. This is called **reintroduction**. These projects look at the whole ecosystem. They consider climate change. They involve Indigenous people and local knowledge. Plant experts work with governments. Businesses and organizations help, too. It's a community effort. Communities around the world are restoring nature.

The Native Plant Trust worked to restore plants on Cadillac Mountain. This mountain is in Acadia National Park in Maine. More than 500,000 people visit every year. All those feet trample plants and soil. The Native Plant Trust studied the mountain. They learned what kinds of plants grow there. They saw how climate change affected the plants. They tested which planting methods worked best. Then they continued to monitor the project. They hope it can be repeated on other mountains.

◀ Some communities encourage people to skip mowing in the month of May. "No Mow May" helps bees and other insects that are becoming active after winter.

SPEAK UP FOR NATIVE PLANTS

People across the country want to get rid of lawns. They want native plants instead. Native plants are better for water and air. They benefit wildlife and communities. But some communities have rules that require neat lawns.

Find out if your local government has rules about lawns. Write a letter about why native plants are important. Tell them you want more biodiversity in your community. Ask them to support native plants instead of lawns.

There are lots of ways your local government can save native plants. They can stop using pesticides. They can use native plants in landscaping. They can encourage people to replace their lawns. People can plant native grasses. Or they can create gardens with lots of different wildflowers and plants. Even mowing less and letting noninvasive weeds grow can help.

Native plants can be used to replace grass lawns near roadsides, schools, and other buildings.

Include these suggestions in your letter. Add your own ideas to help native plants. Ask your friends to sign your letter. Your teacher and parents can sign, too. This shows that lots of people support native plants. Send the letter to your mayor or town council.

CREATE A NATIVE PLANT PLAN FOR YOUR SCHOOL

Schools often have landscaping around their buildings. These are places where native plants can live.

Here's how you can make a plan for native plants at your school:

1 Create a map of the school property. Include all the places where there's grass. Include flower beds and shrubs.

2 Mark the places where native plants could be planted. Sports fields need to have grass. But patches of lawn near the playground or sidewalks could be replaced. Ask your principal if there are already any native plants around the school.

3 Research native plants in your area. Make a list of ideas for what could be planted. Color in areas where native grasses can be planted. Use a different color to show where wildflower gardens can go. You can also include an organic vegetable garden. Classes could learn to grow food.

4. Write down why native plants are important. Write how native plants can teach people about biodiversity. Include the importance of not using pesticides on lawns and flowers.

5. Present your plan to your teacher. Ask if your class can create a garden. You can start with one small area. You can plant organic vegetables or native plants. Your class can learn about biodiversity.

Your teacher will have to get permission from the principal or school board before starting any project. Offer to help present your idea. You can also make a plan for your home. Show it to your parents. Ask them to help you grow native plants.

A school garden can promote the growth of native plants and encourage biodiversity.

LEARN MORE

Loh-Hagan, Virginia. *Indigenous Rights*. Ann Arbor, MI: Cherry Lake Publishing, 2022.

Silverthorne, Elizabeth. *Plants*. Ann Arbor, MI: Cherry Lake Publishing, 2009.

Tallamy, Douglas W. *Nature's Best Hope (Young Readers' Edition): How You Can Save the World in Your Own Yard*. Portland, OR: Timber Press, 2023.

Vonder Brink, Tracy. *Protecting the Amazon Rainforest*. Lake Elmo, MN: Focus Readers, 2020.

GLOSSARY

agriculture (AA-grih-kuhl-chuhr) the business of how people grow crops

biodiversity (by-oh-duh-VUHR-suh-tee) the variety of plants and animals in nature

botany (BAH-tuh-nee) the scientific study of plants

climate change (KLY-muht CHAYNJ) changes in weather, temperatures, and other natural conditions over time

conservation (kahn-suhr-VAY-shuhn) action to protect wildlife and nature

crisis (KRY-suhss) a very difficult time or emergency

deforestation (dee-fohr-uh-STAY-shuhn) the process of cutting down forests

ecosystems (EE-koh-sih-stuhmz) places where plants, animals, and the environment rely on each other

erosion (ih-ROH-zhuhn) when land is worn away by wind or water

extinction (ik-STINK-shuhn) when all of one kind of plant or animal dies

genetic engineering (juh-NEH-tik en-juh-NIHR-ing) a scientific process that changes the inherited traits of a plant or animal

habitat (hah-BUH-tat) the natural home of plants and animals

invasive species (in-VAY-siv spee-SHEEZ) plants or animals that don't belong in an ecosystem

monocultures (MAH-nuh-kuhl-chuhrz) huge fields with one type of crop

native plants (NAY-tiv PLANTZ) plants that are a natural part of an ecosystem

organic (or-GAH-nik) food or other plants grown without toxic chemicals

pesticides (PEH-stuh-sydes) toxic chemicals made to kill a plant or animal that might harm crops

pollinators (PAH-luh-nay-tuhrz) animals that move pollen between plants

reintroduction (ree-ihn-truh-DUHK-shuhn) when plants or animals are brought back to the habitat where they once lived

toxic (TAK-sik) something that is harmful or poisonous

INDEX